This book belongs to:

....

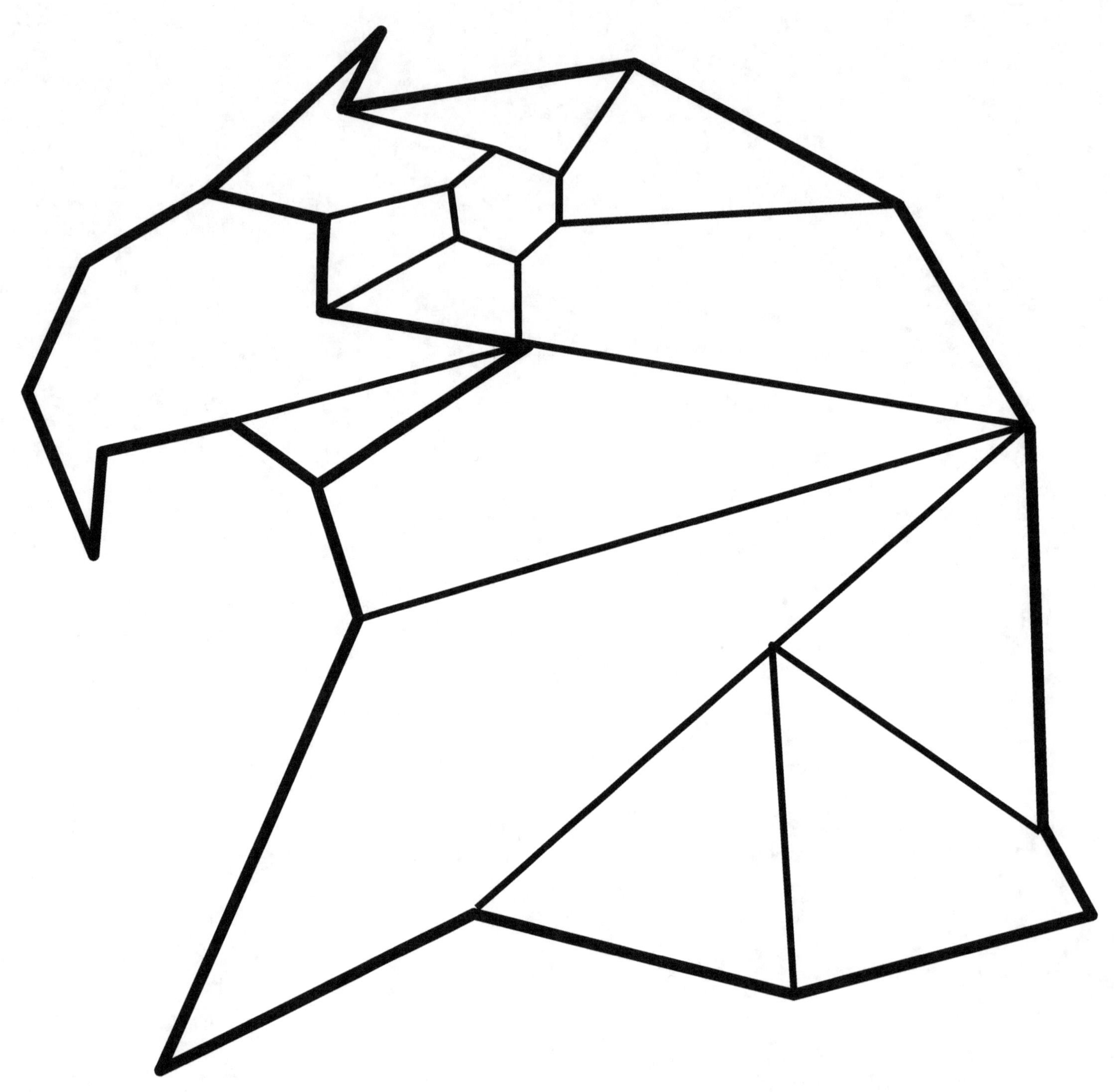

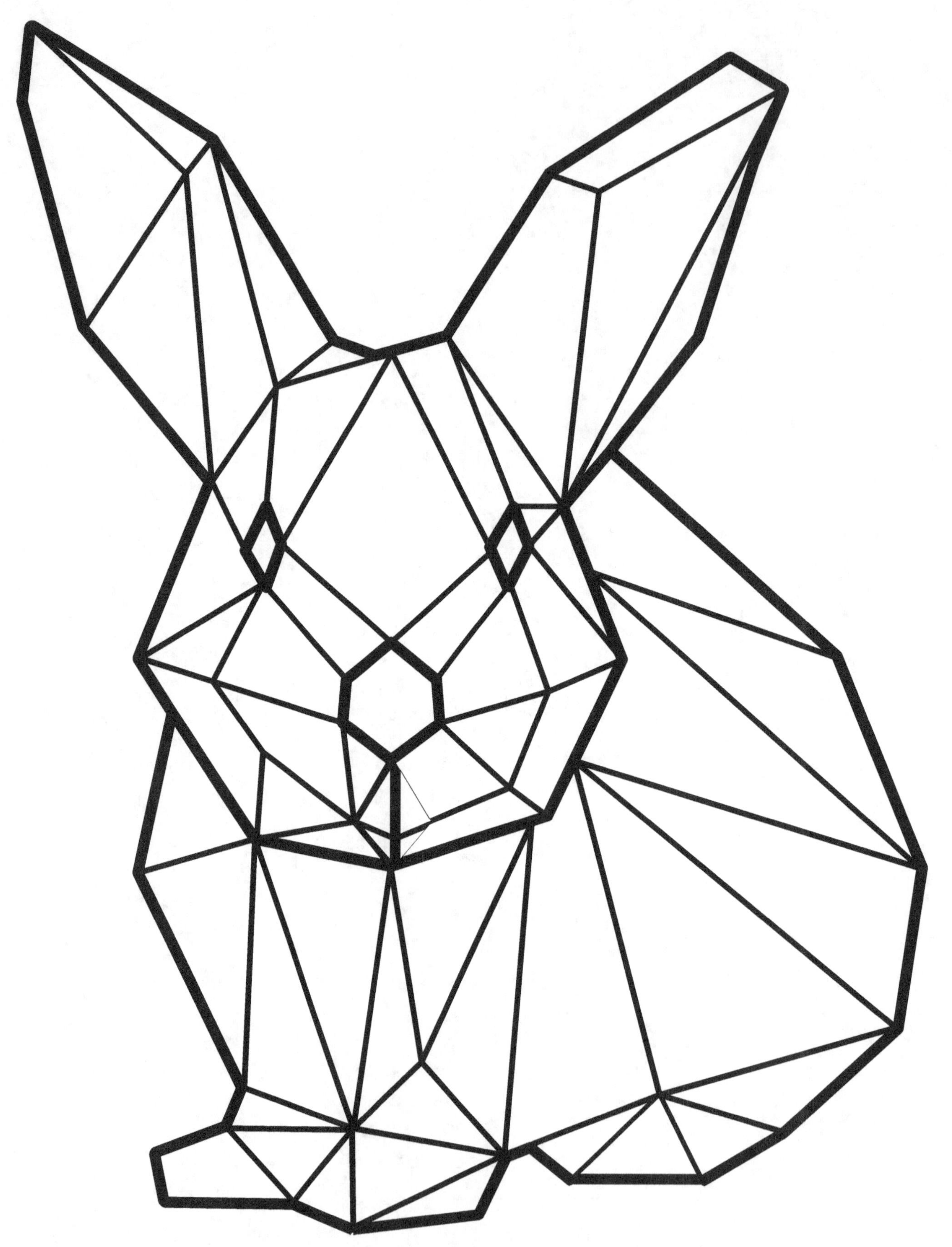

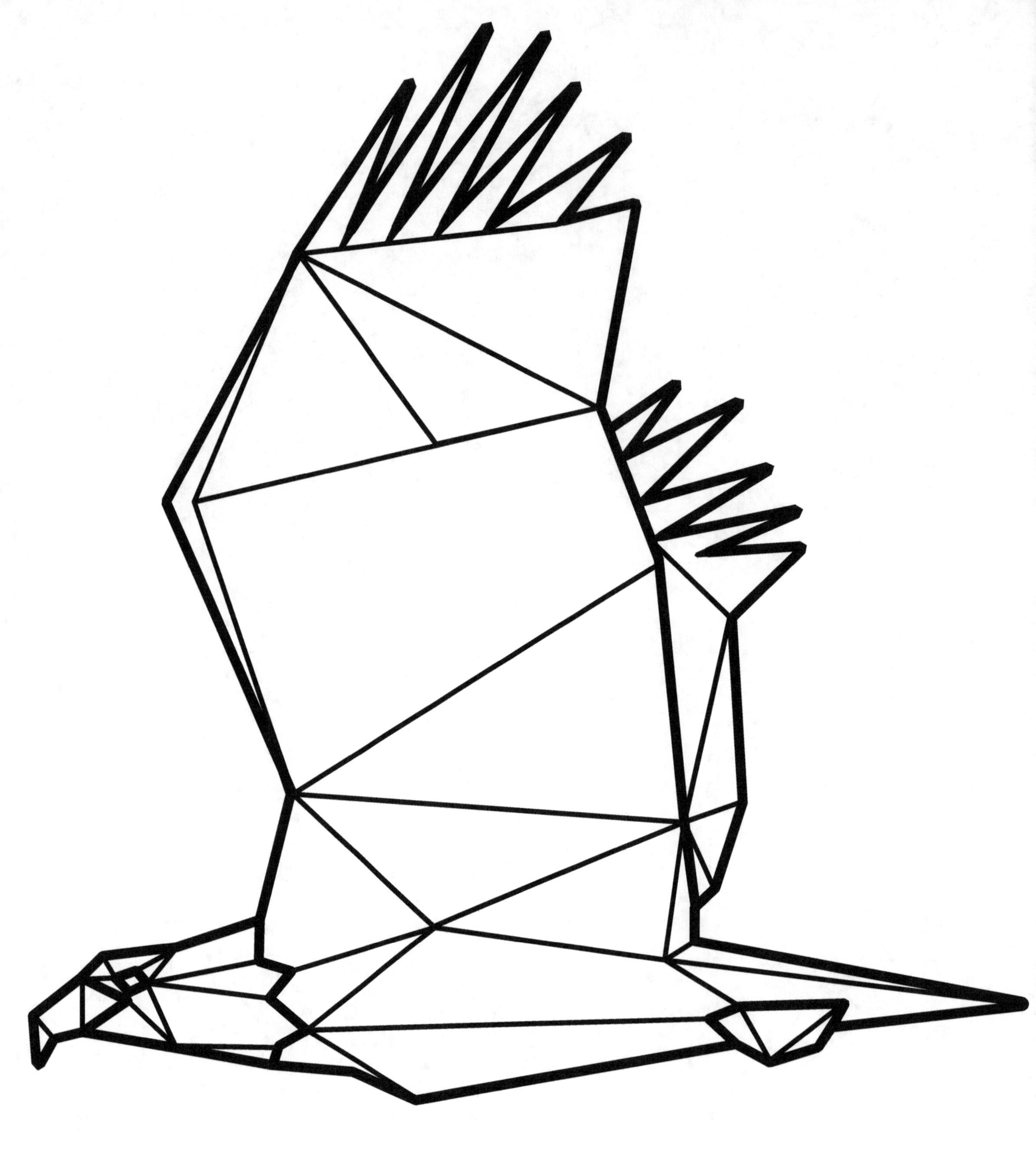

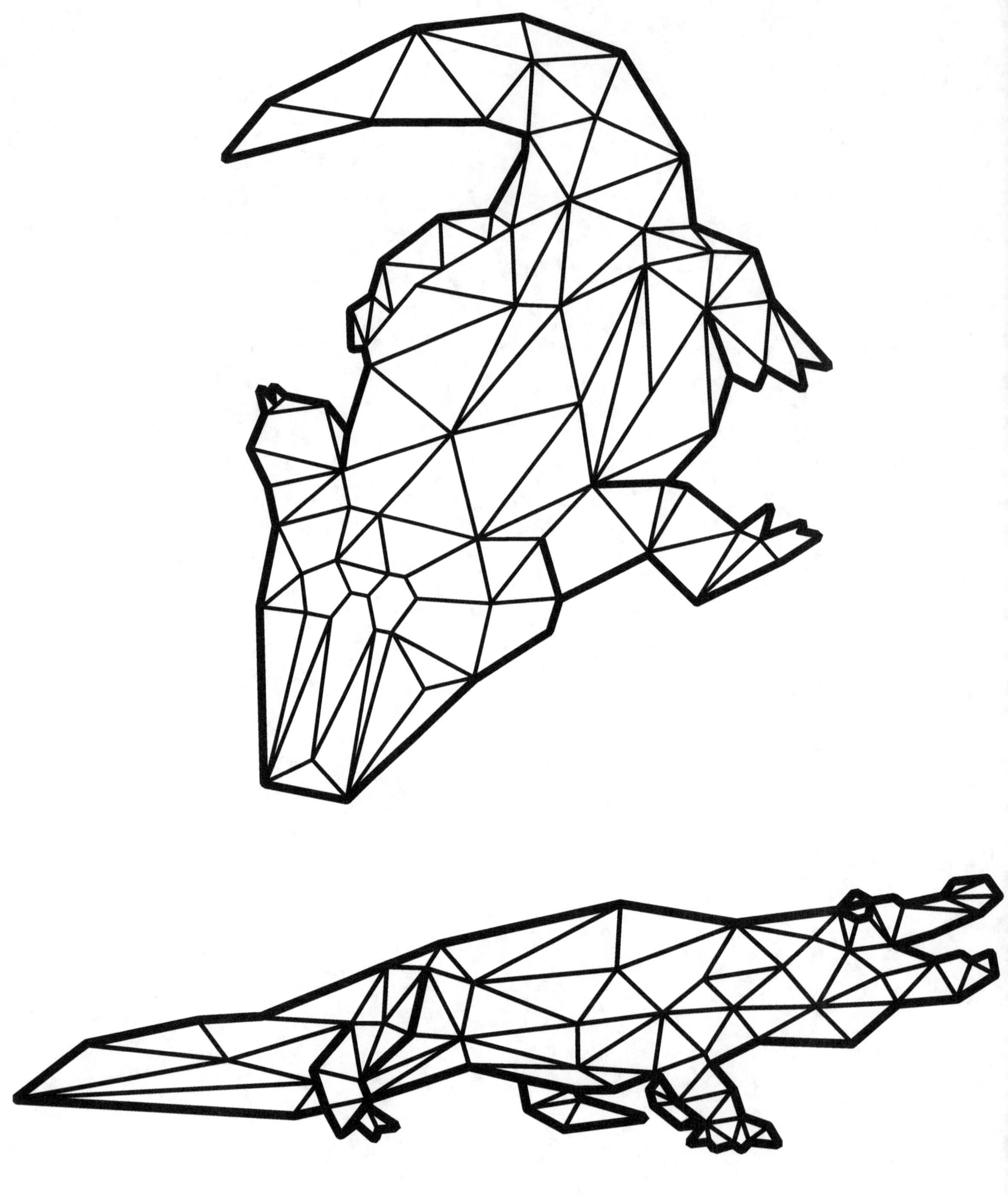

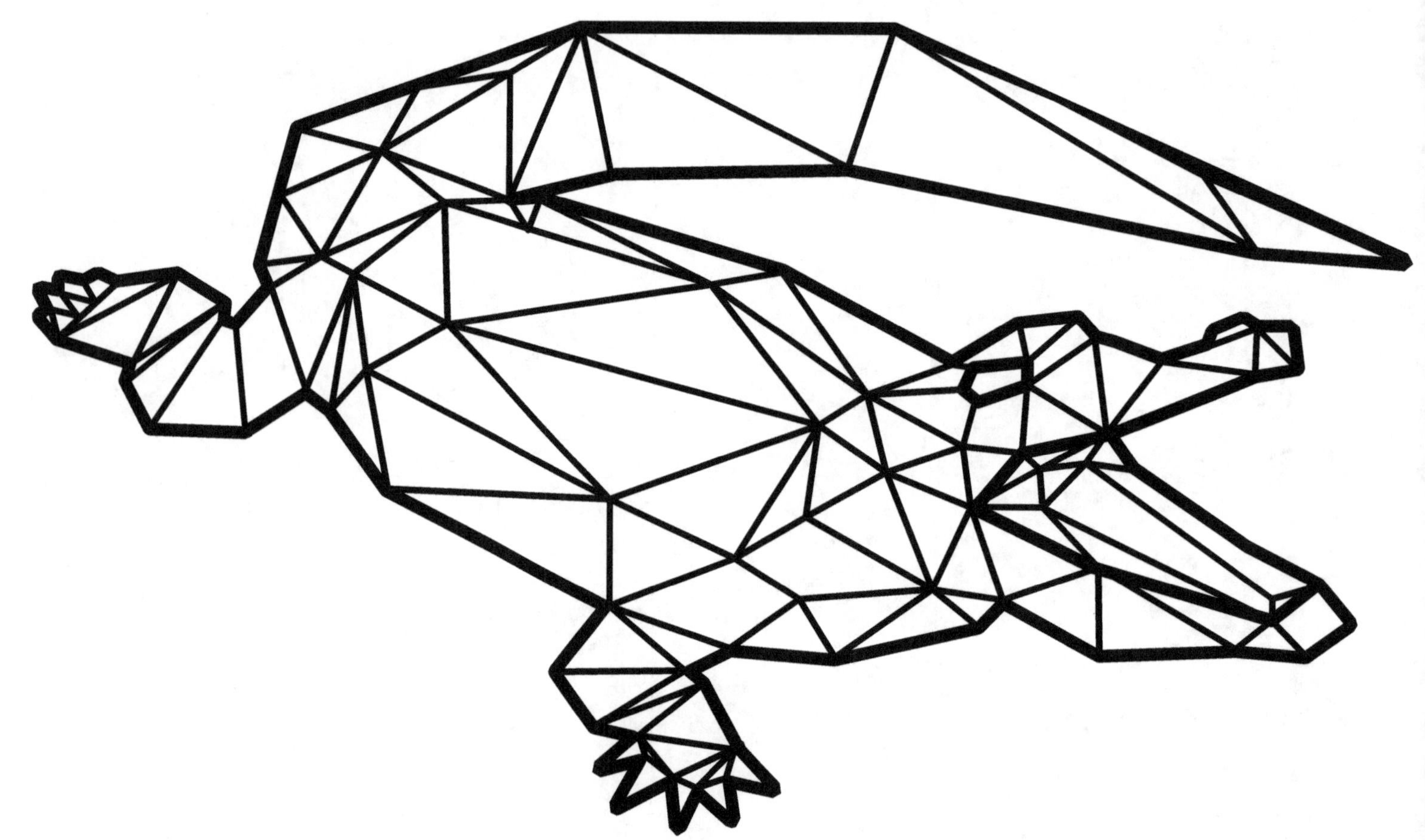

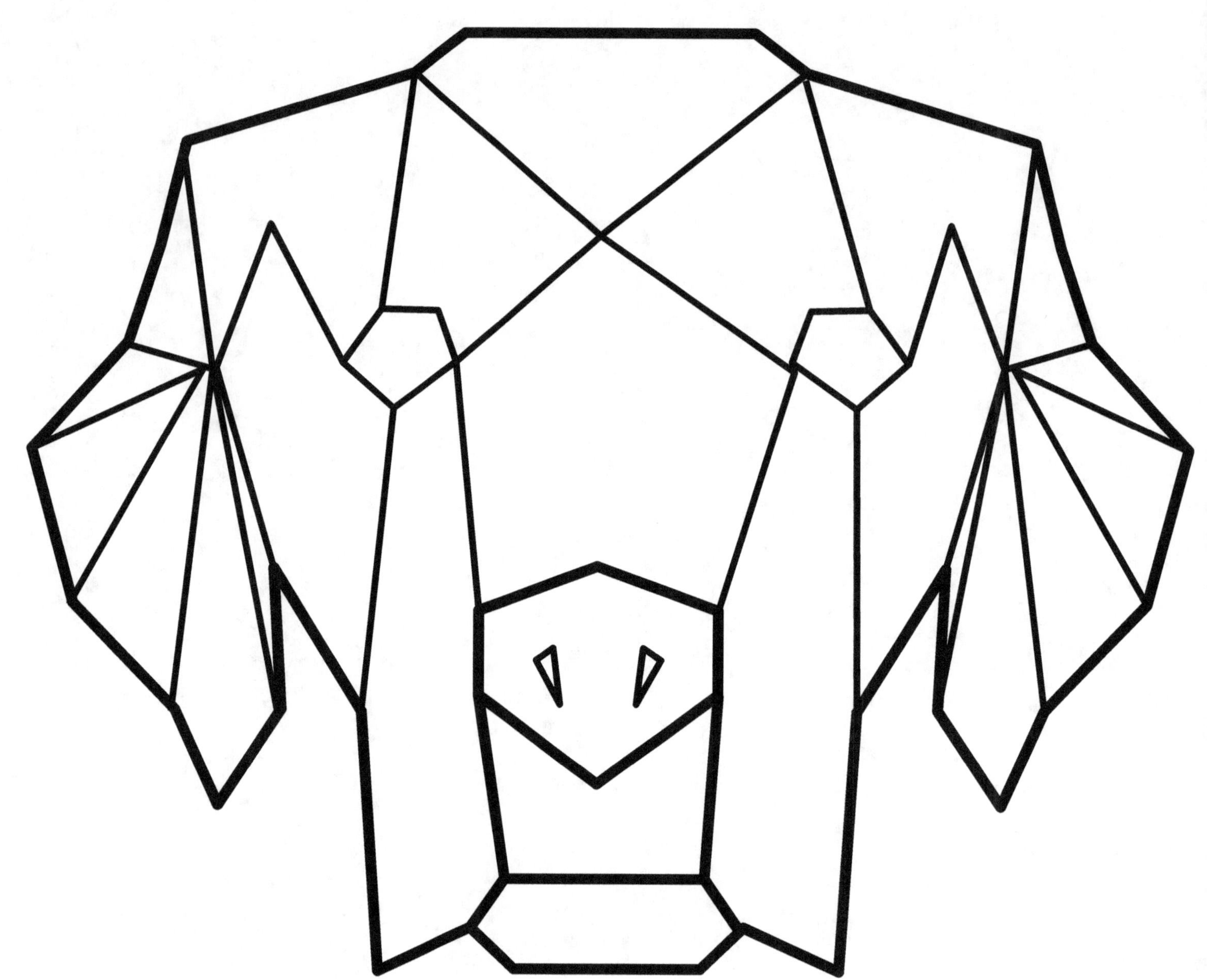

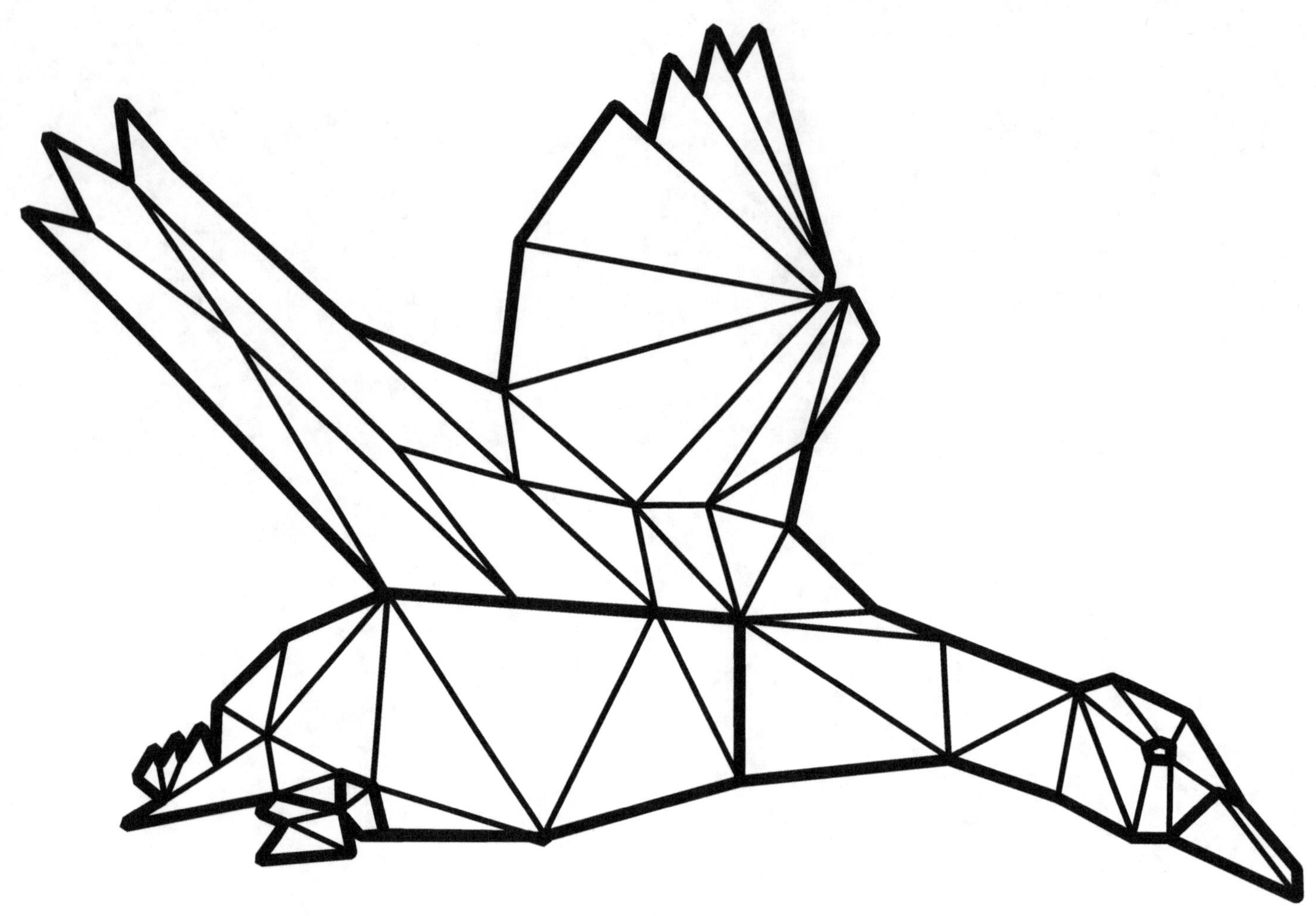

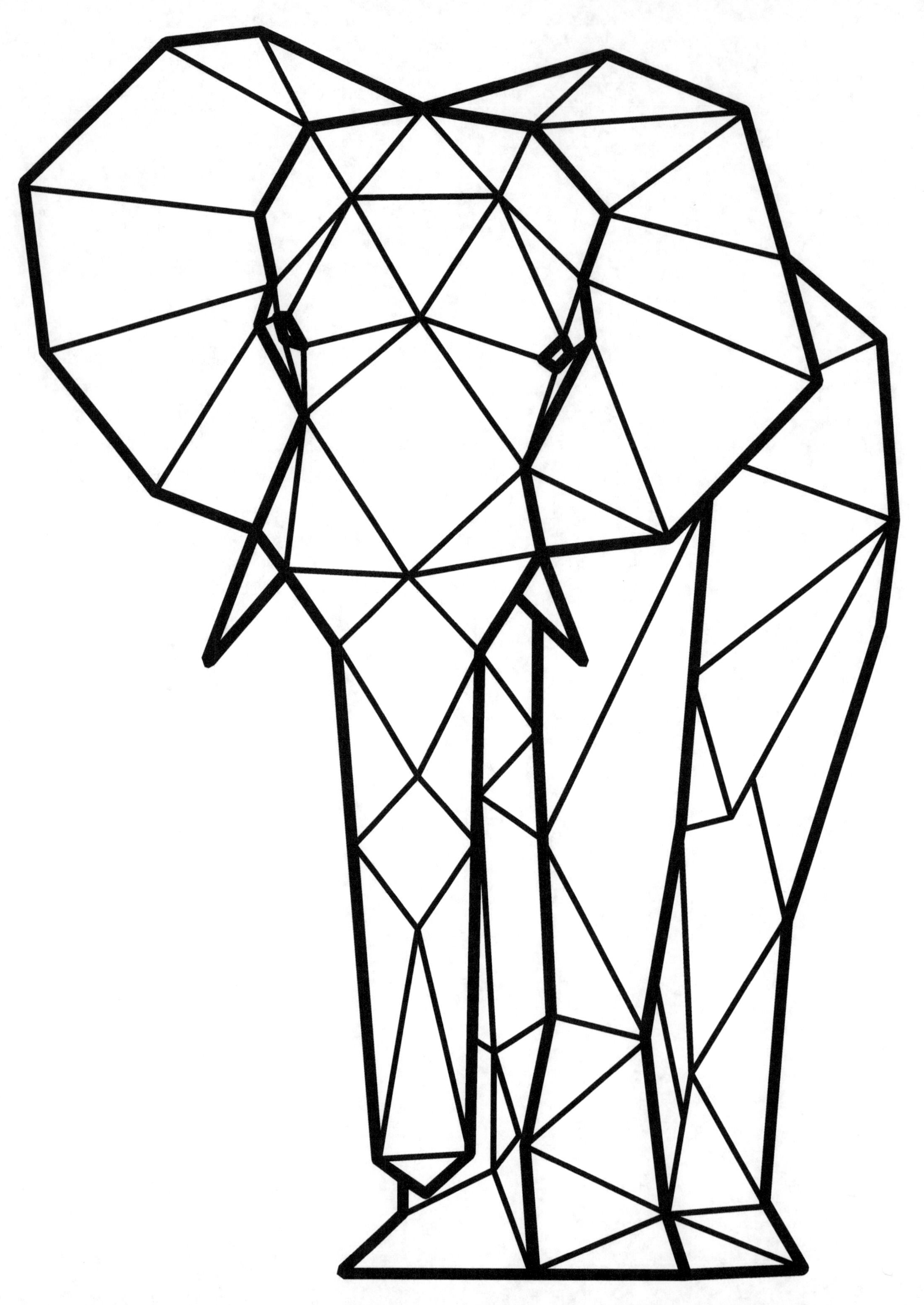

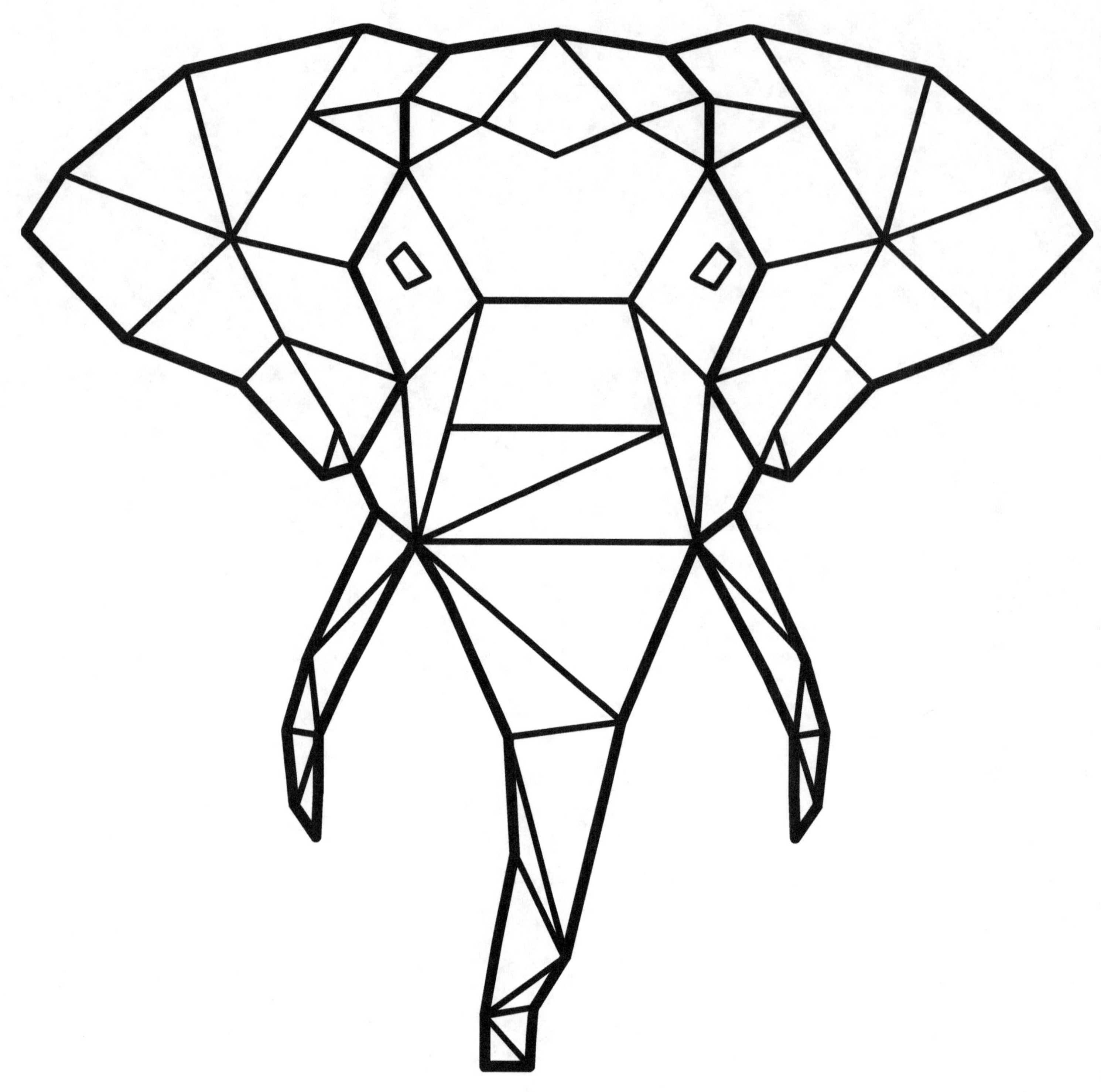

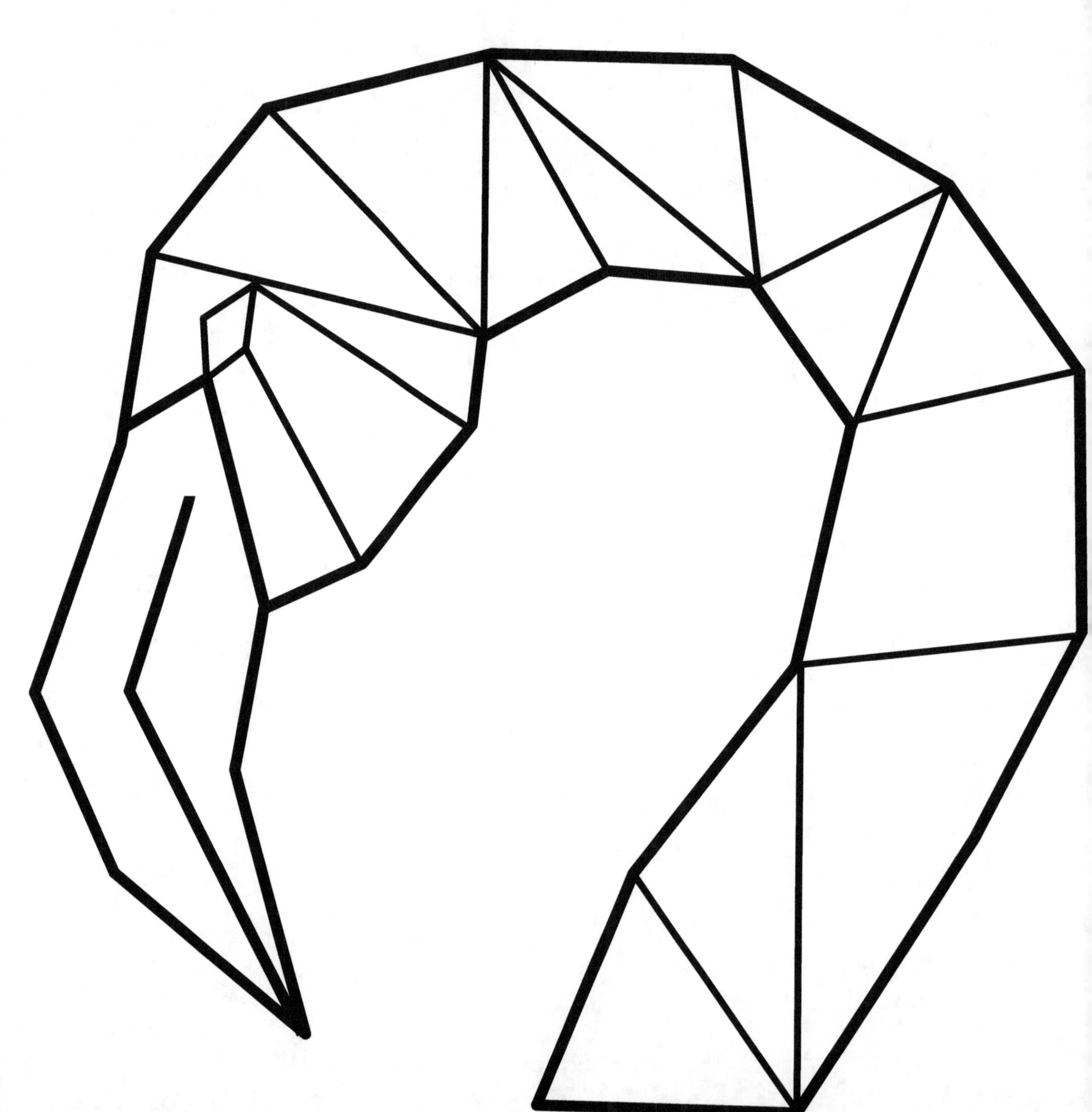

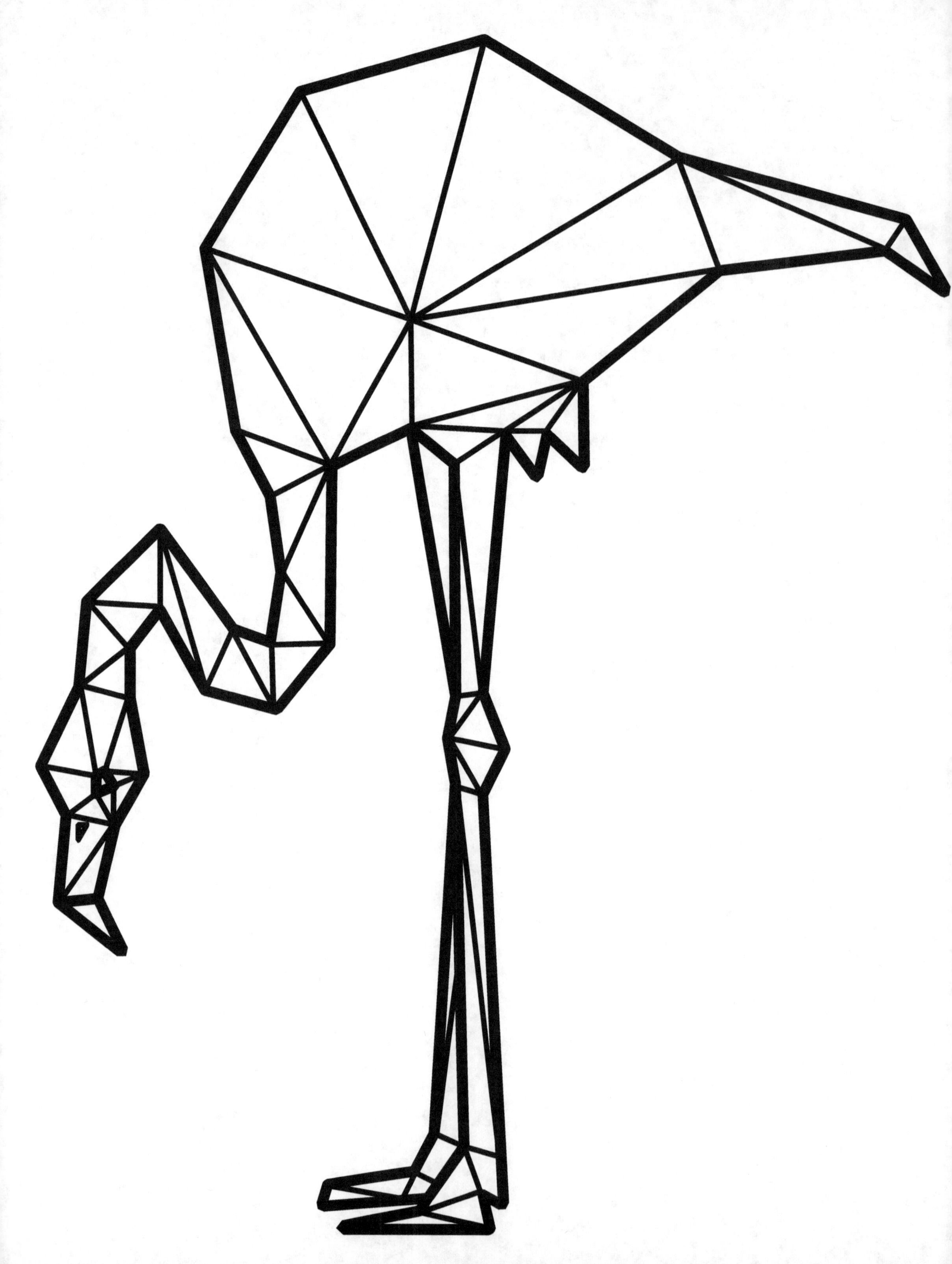

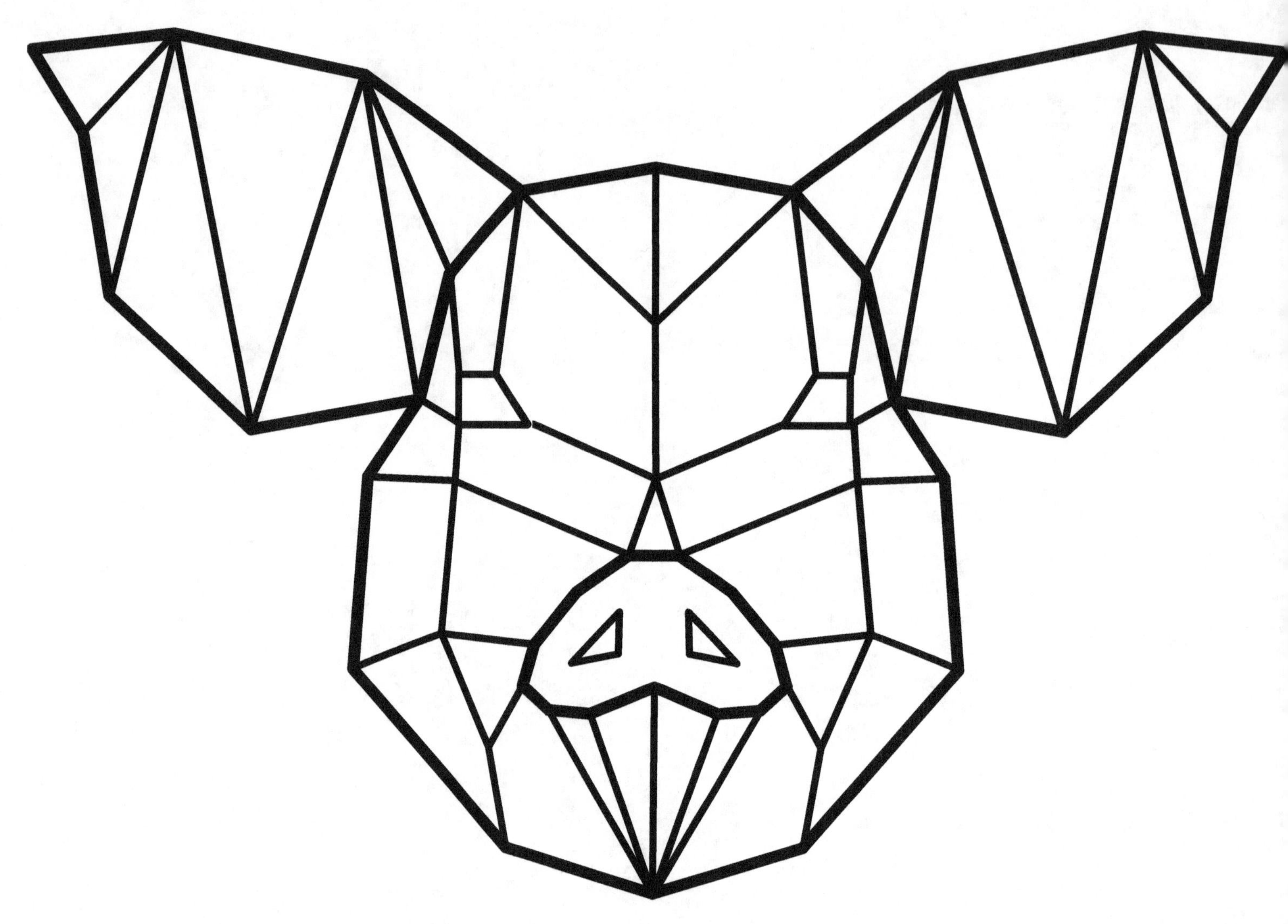

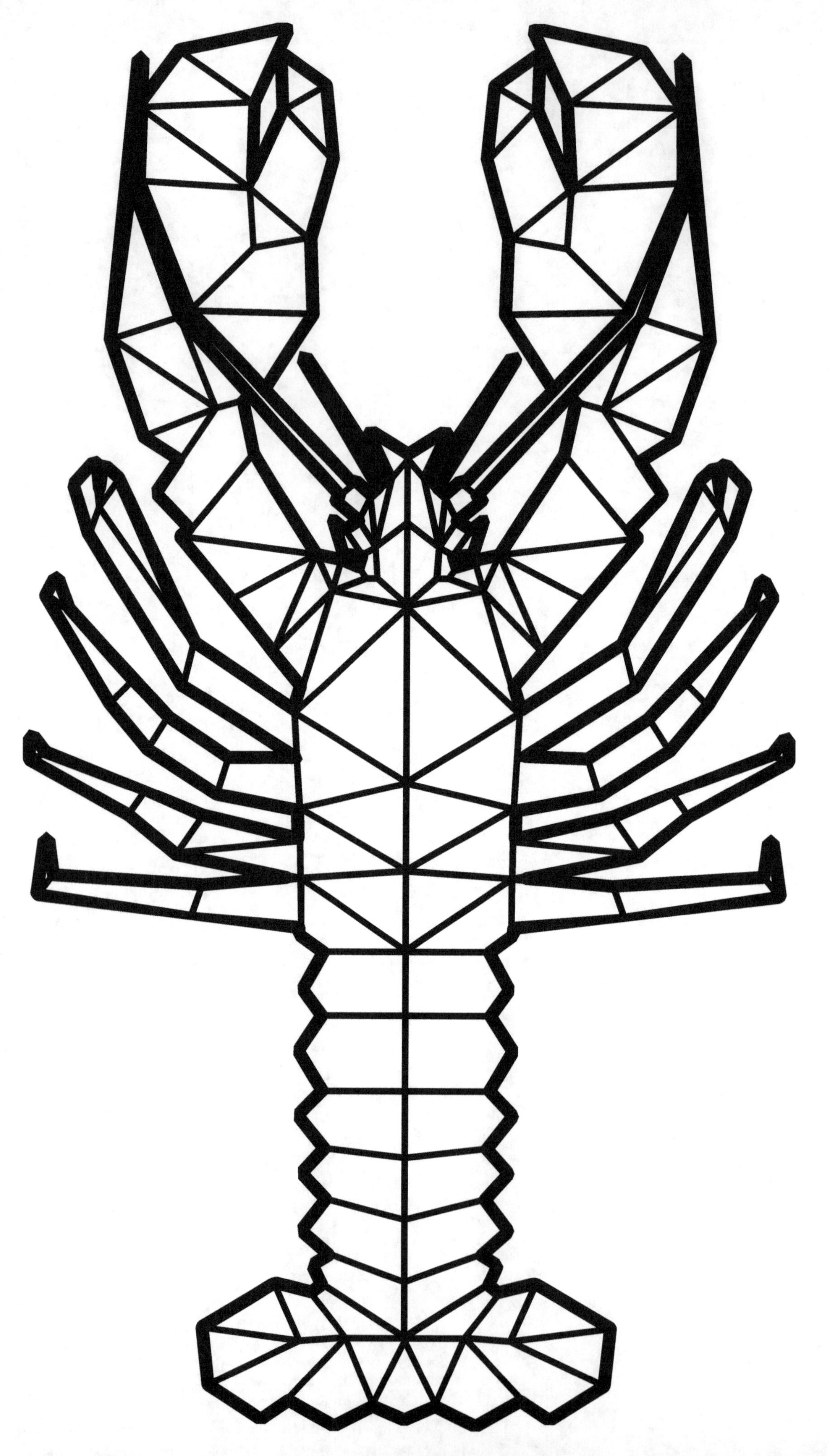

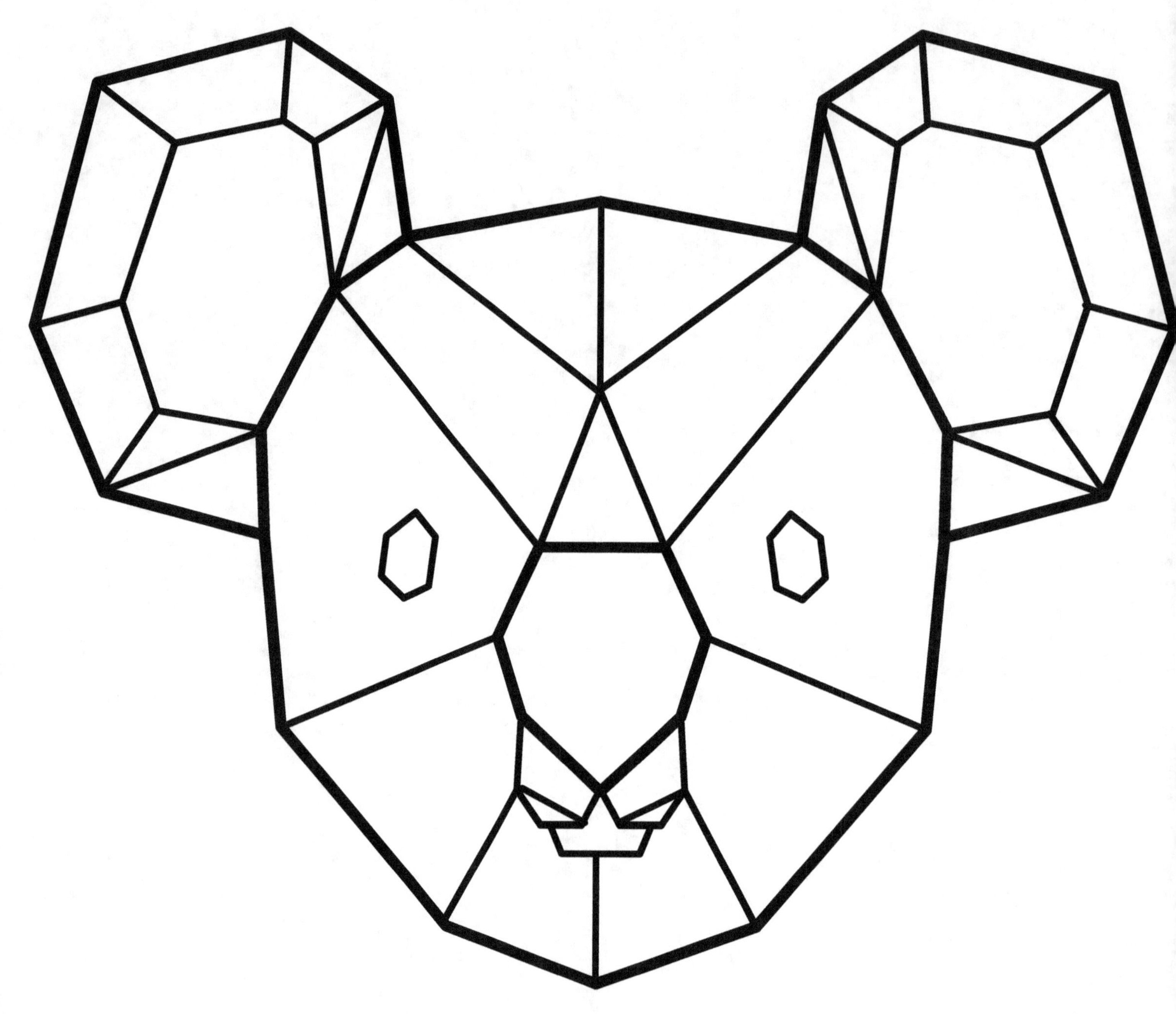

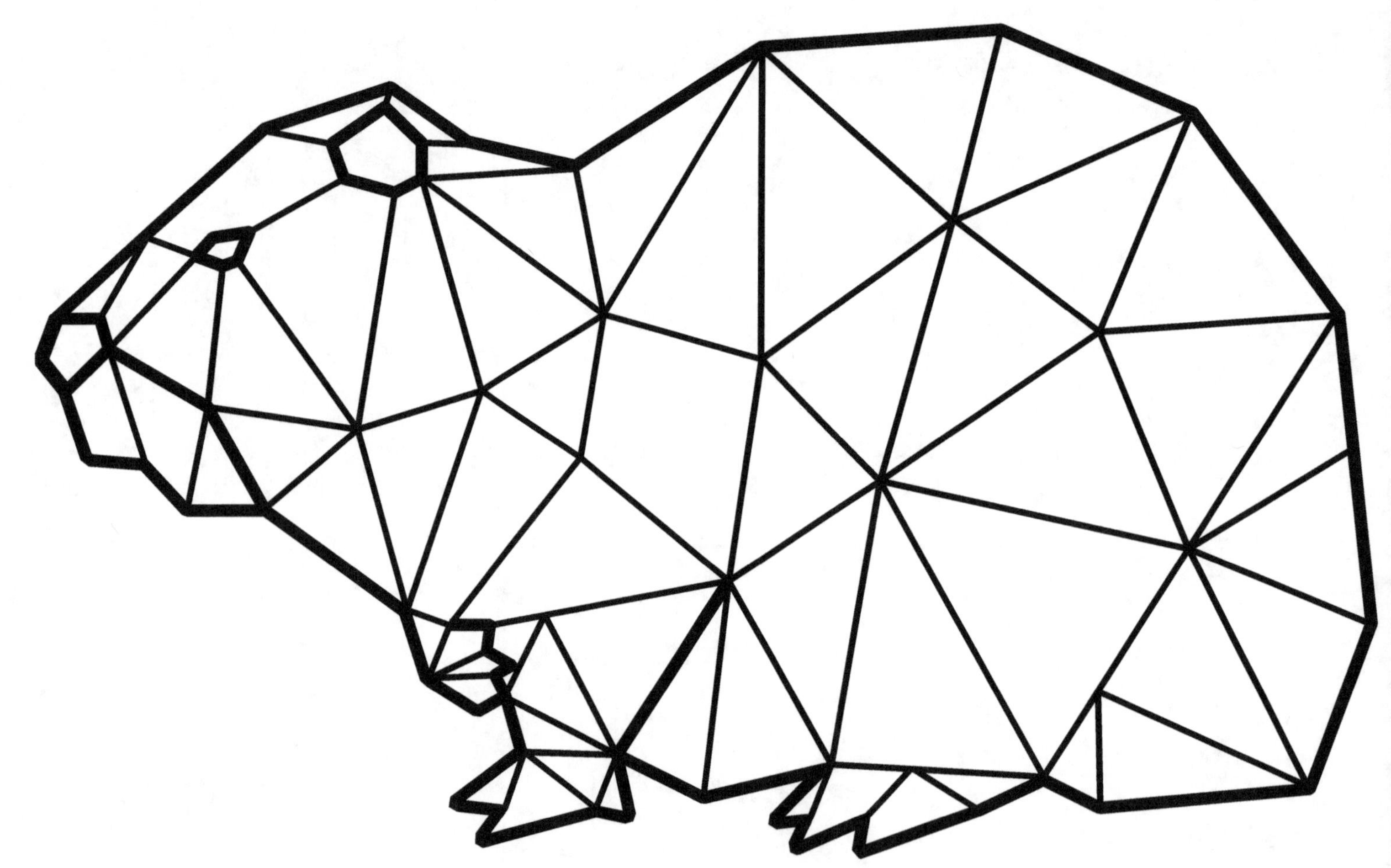

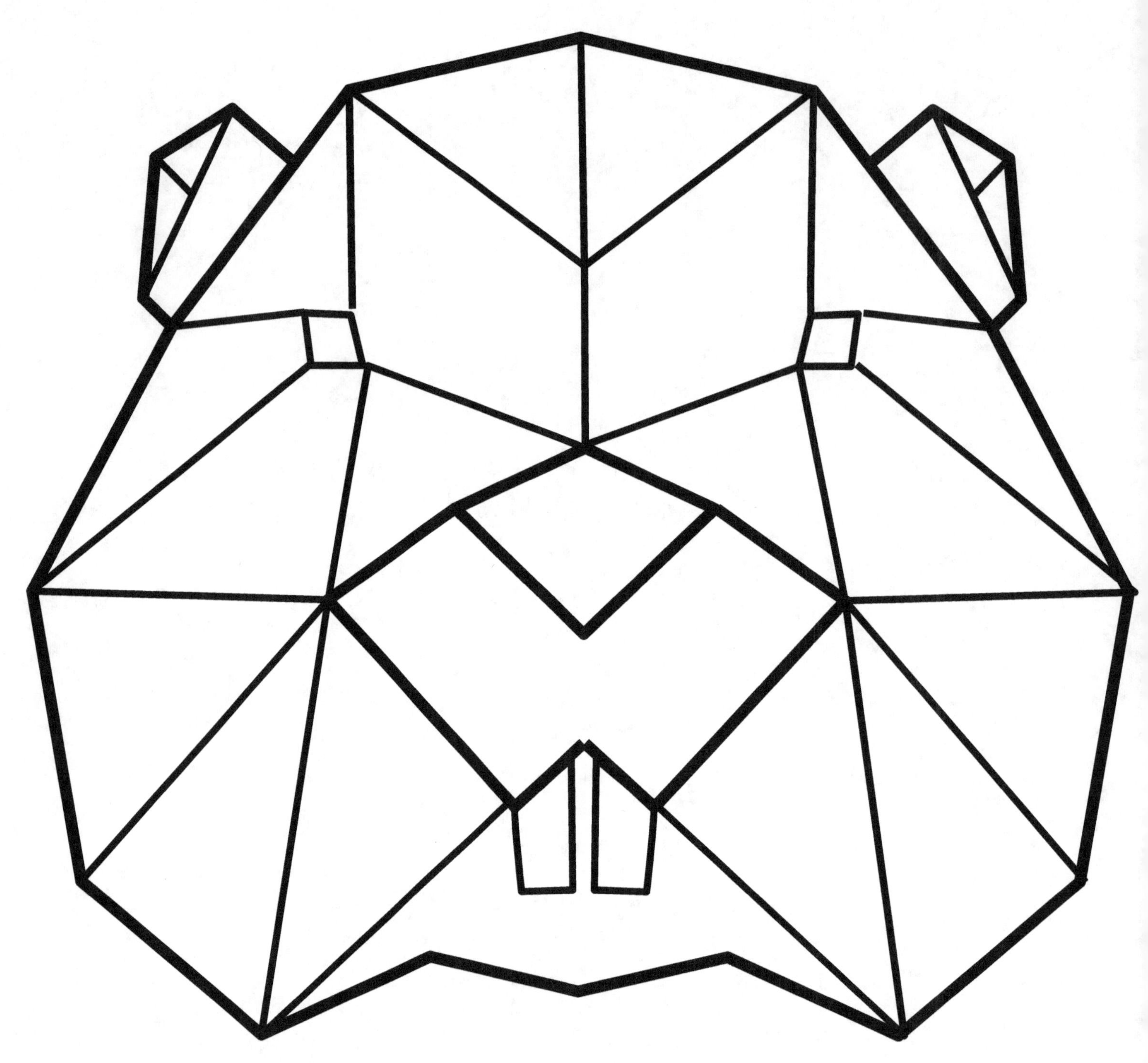

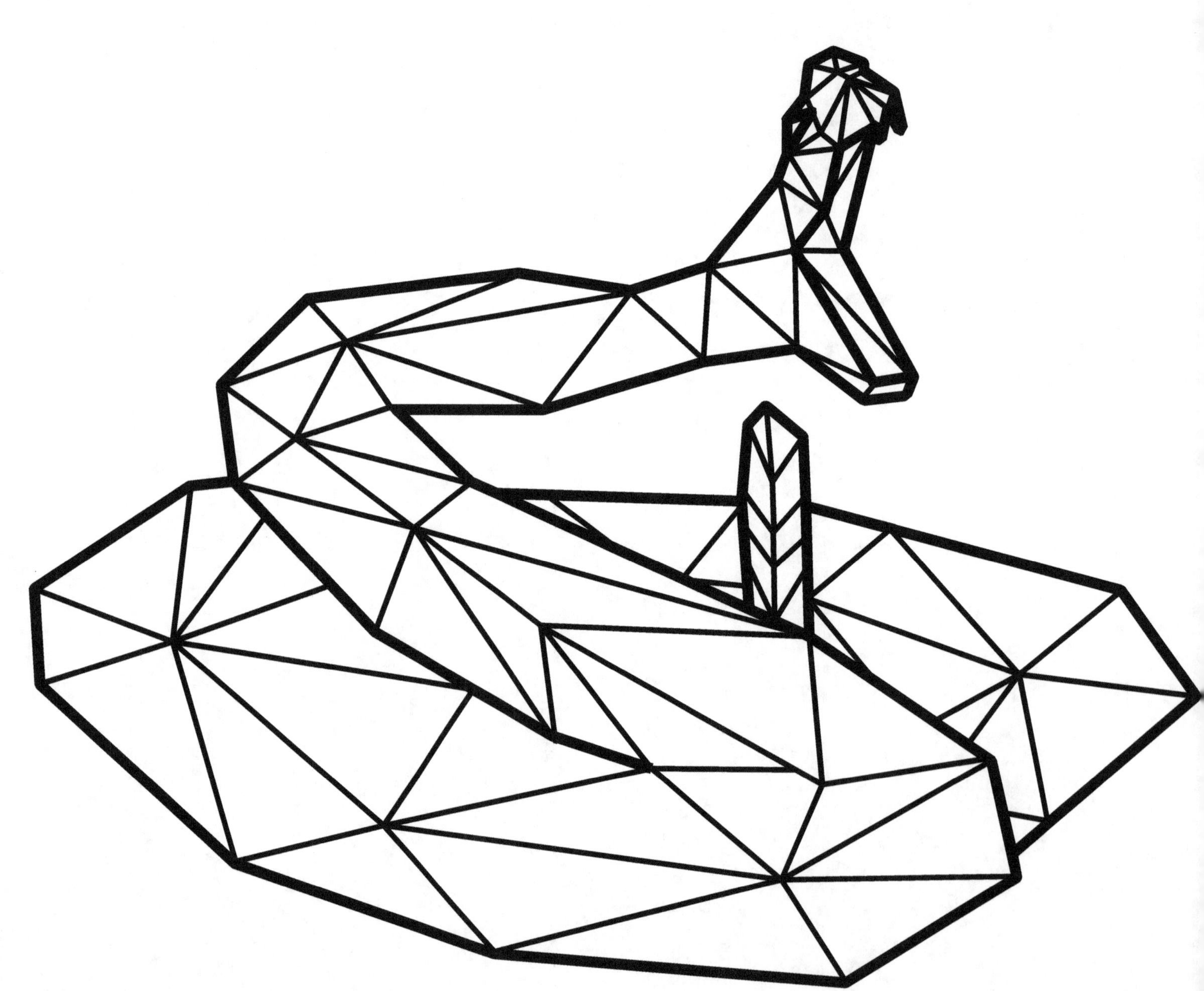

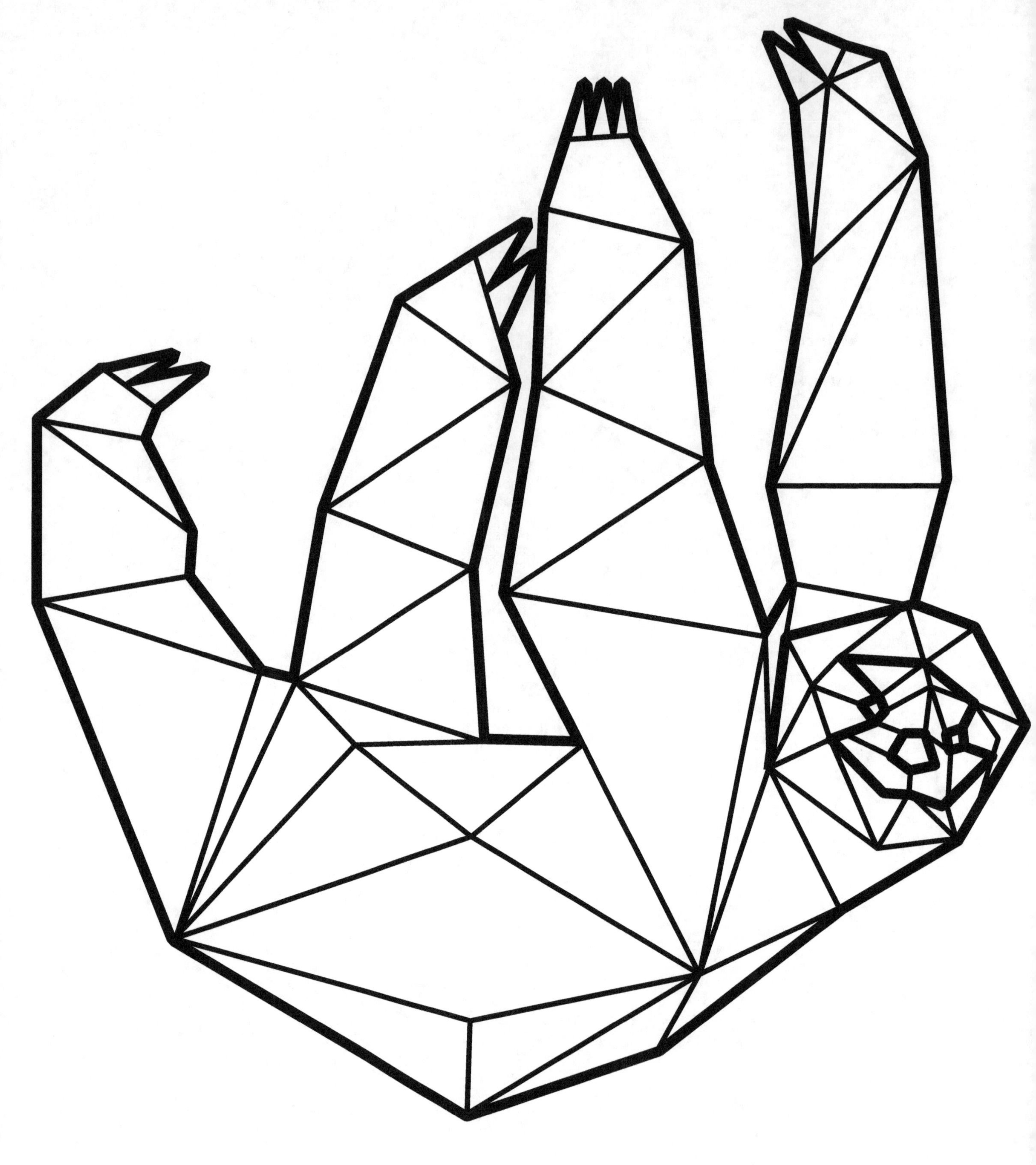

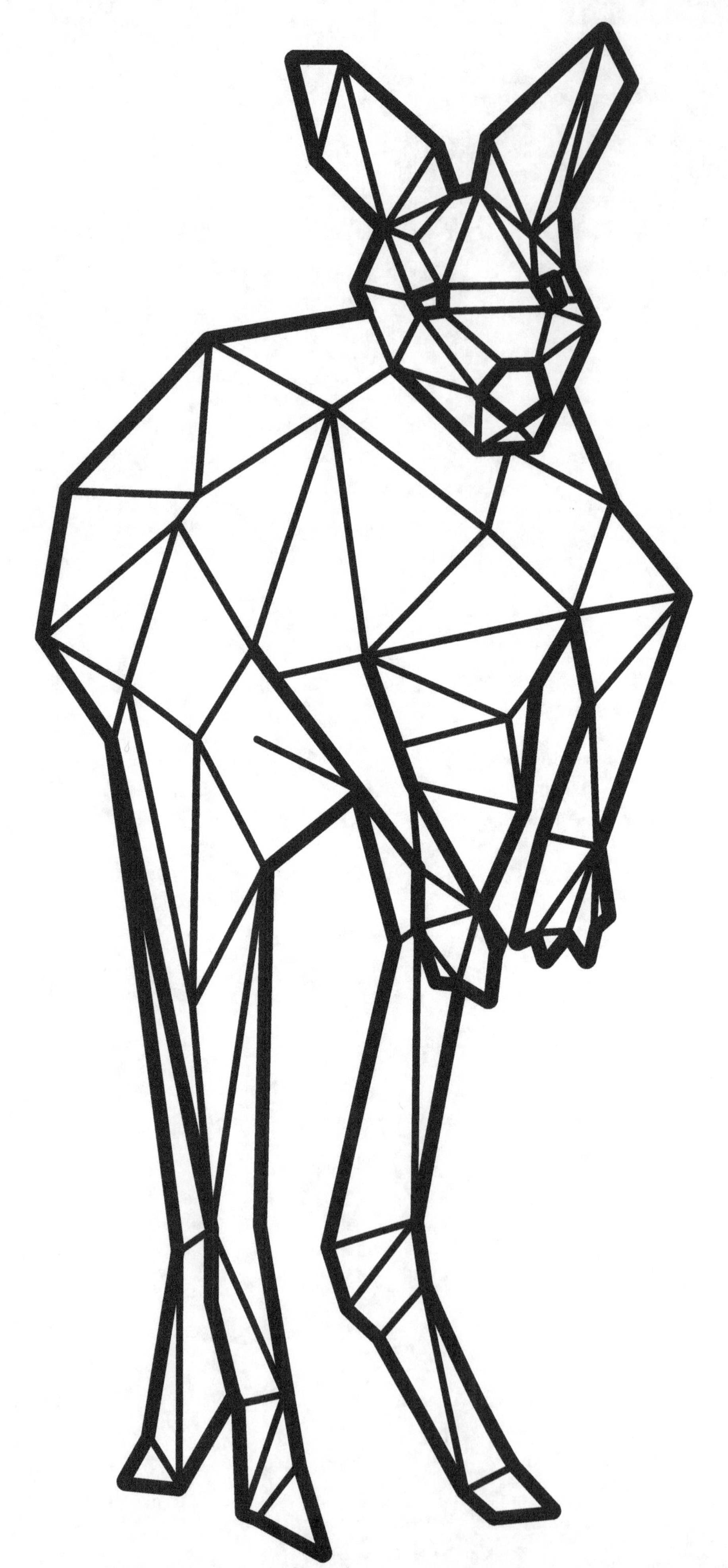

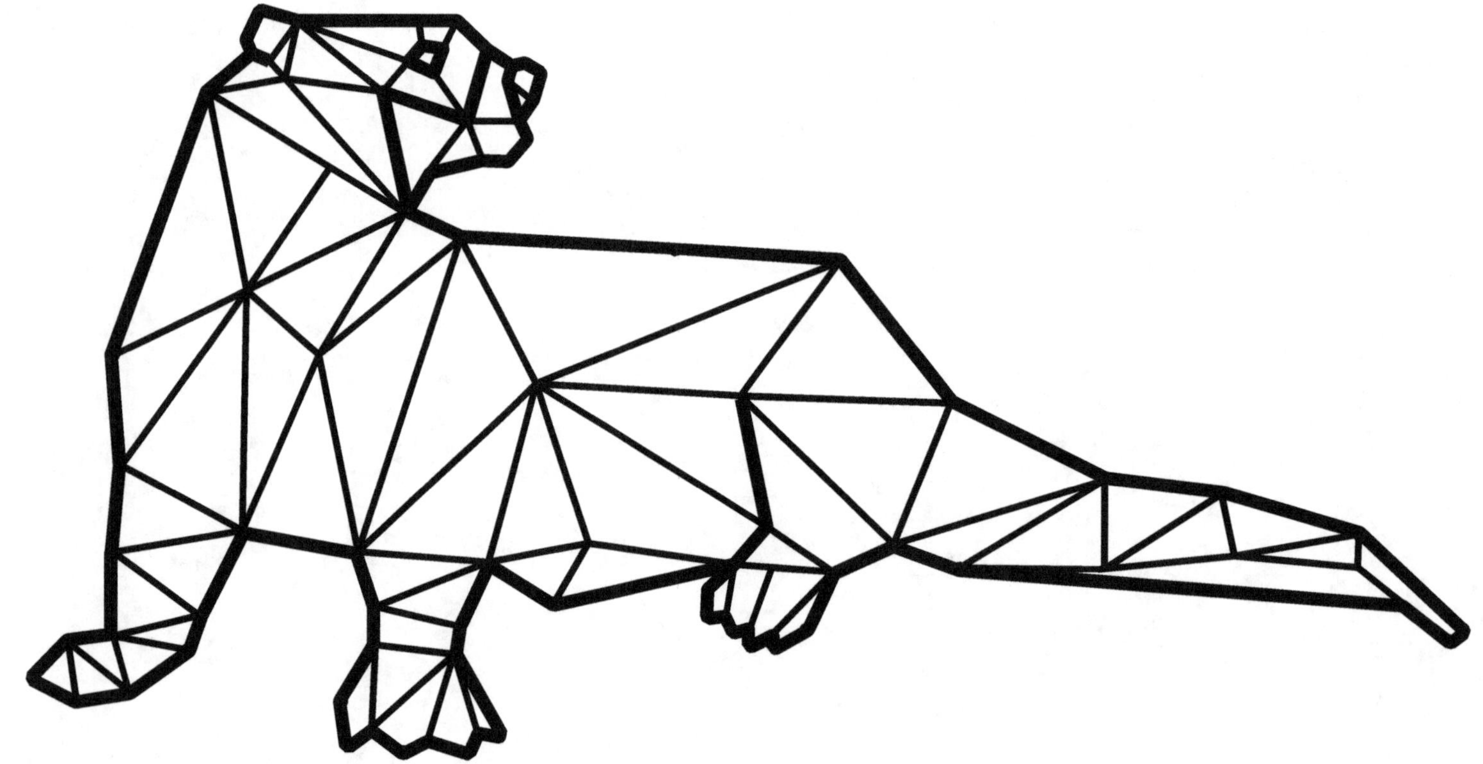

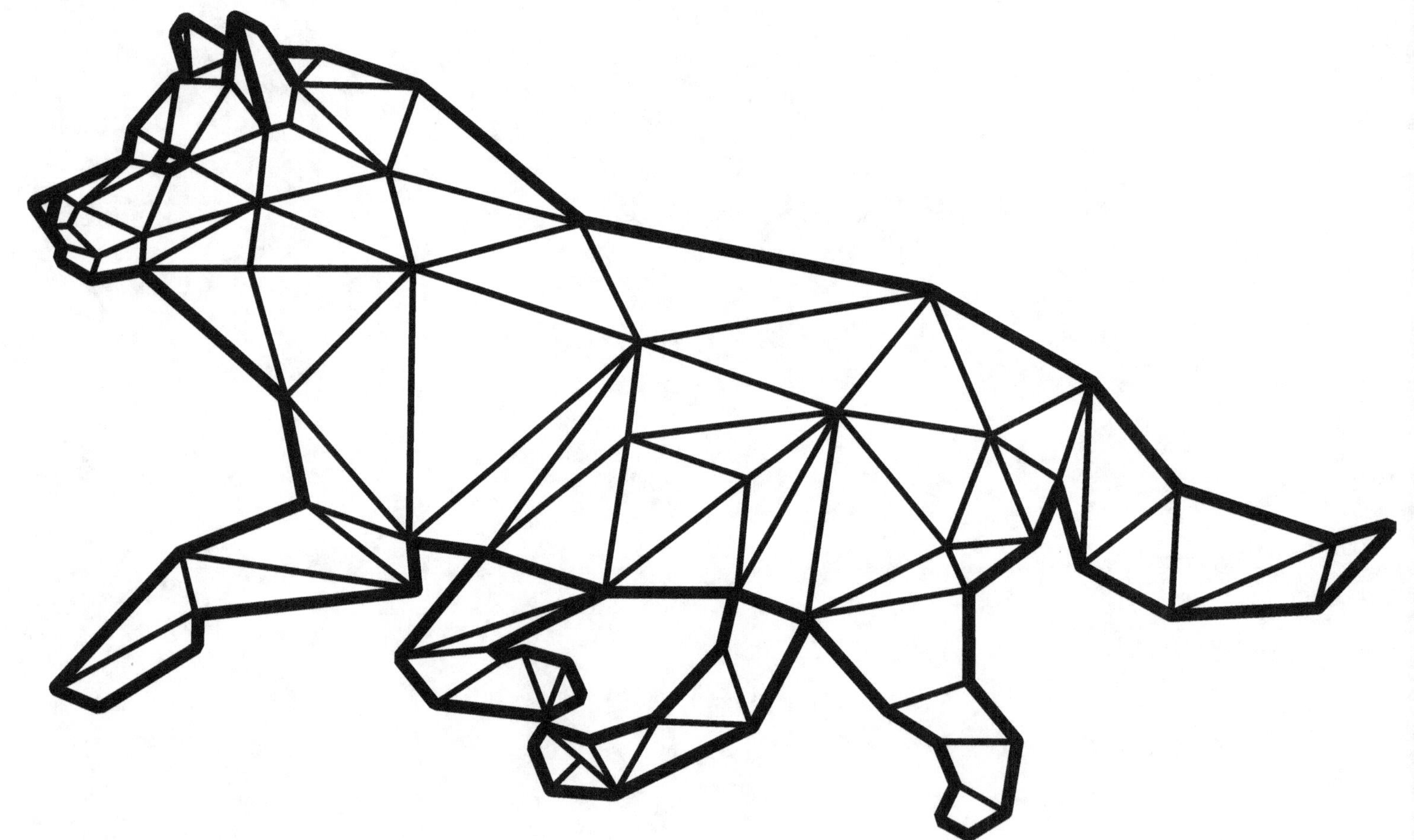

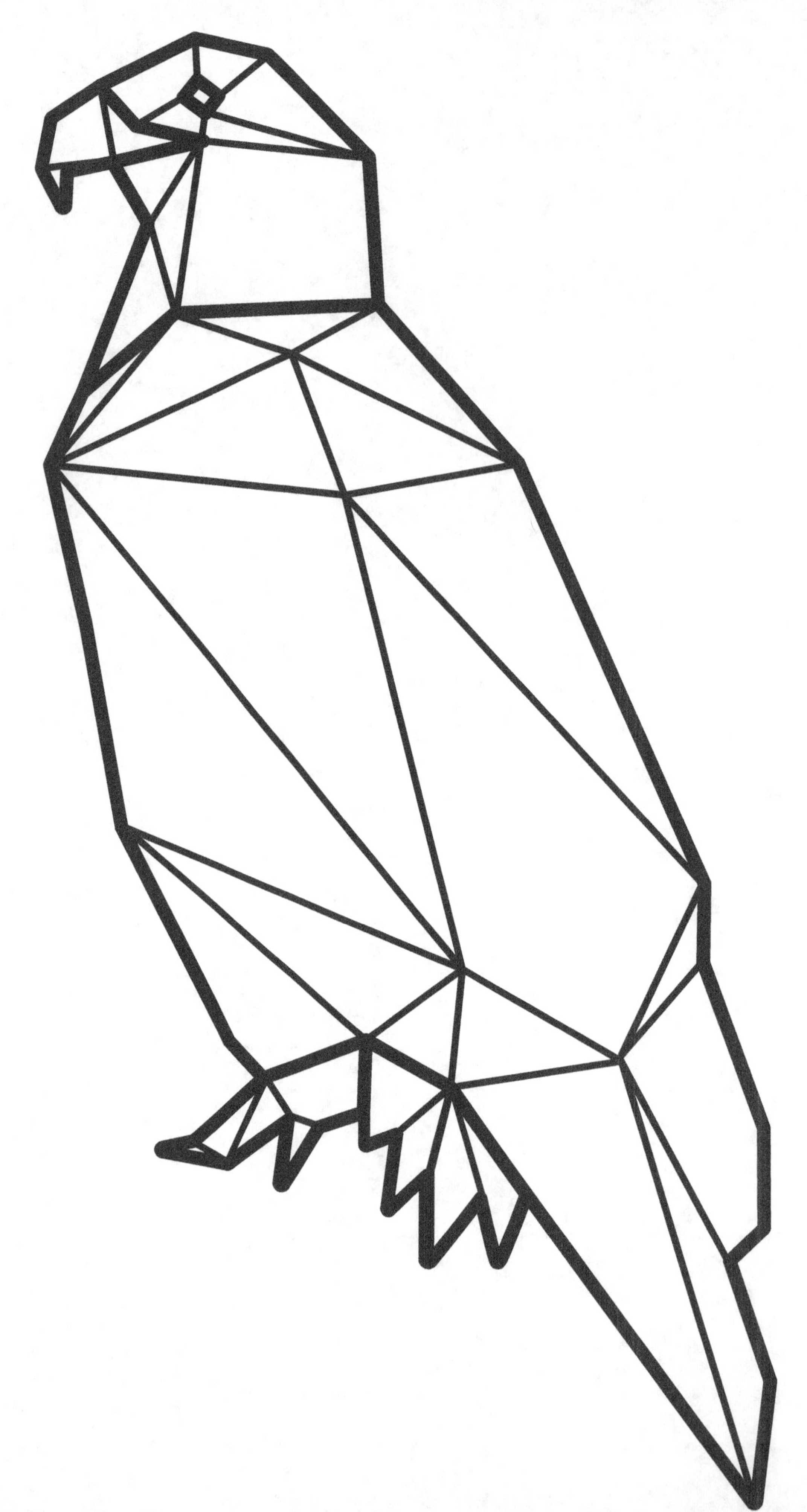

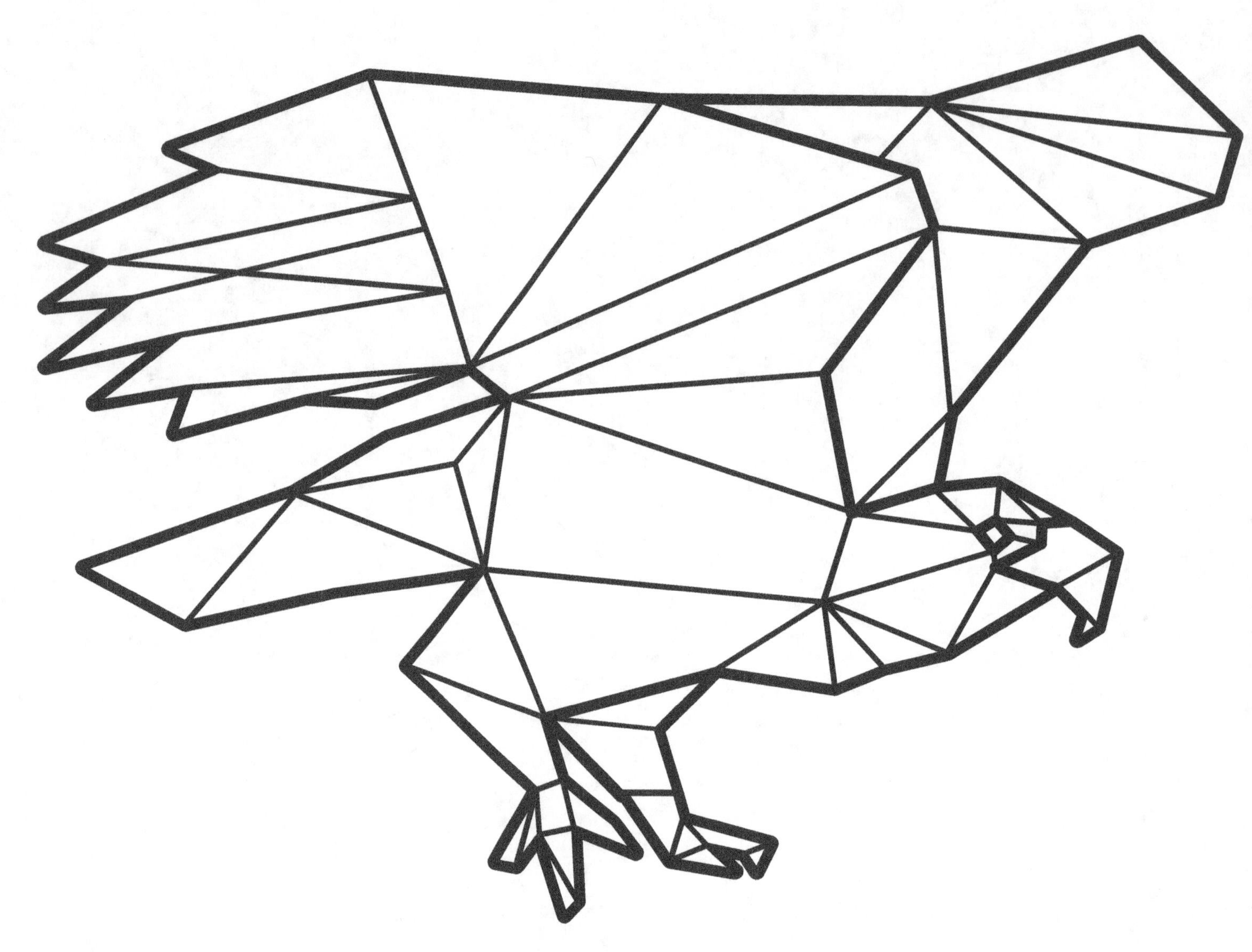

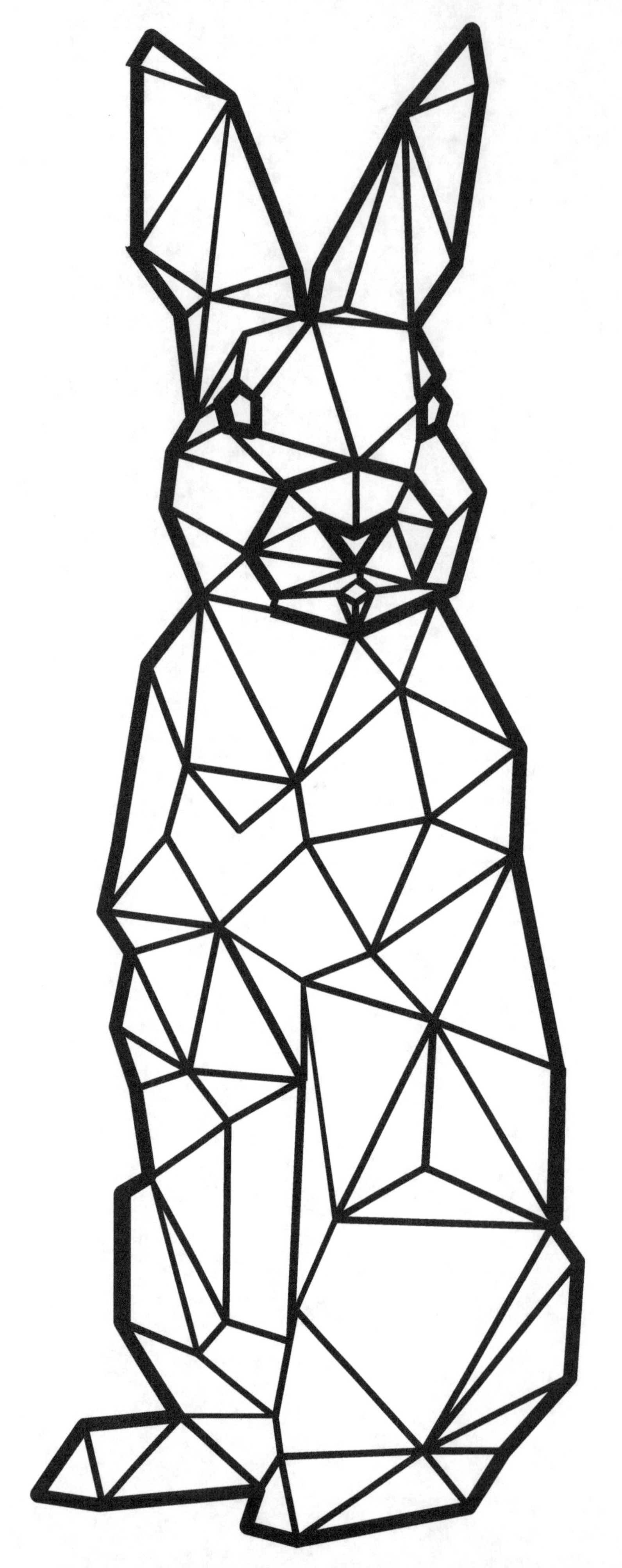

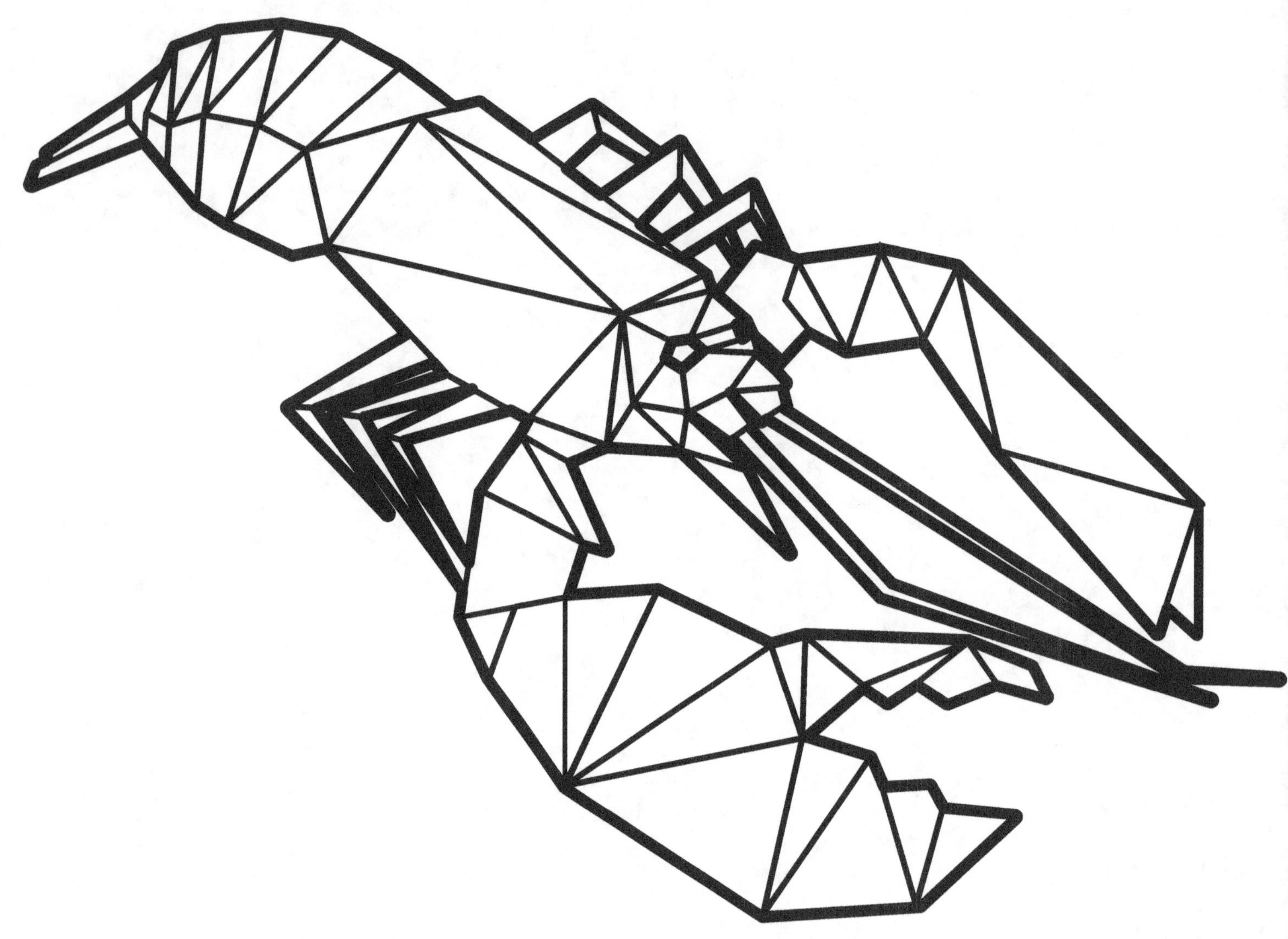

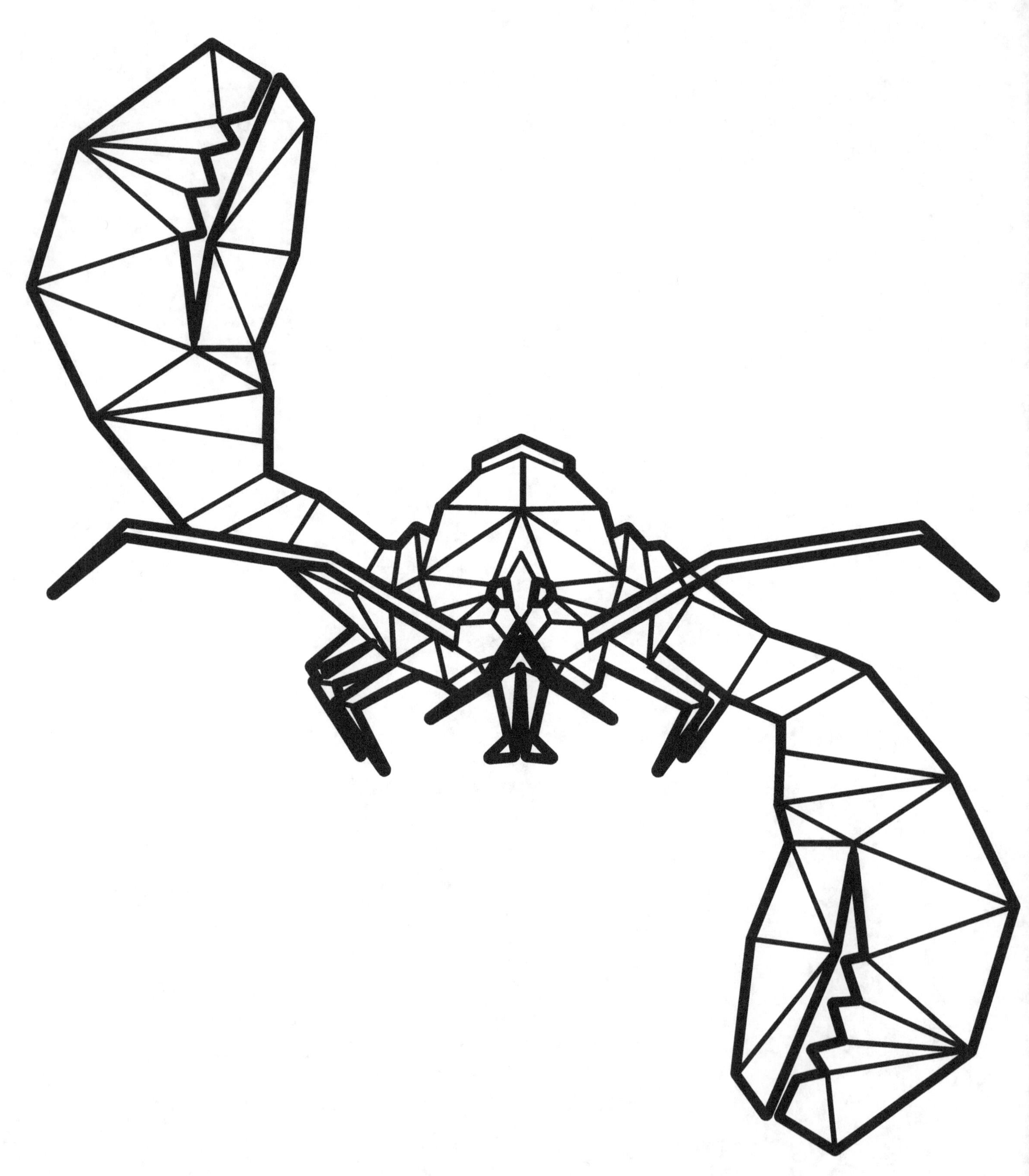

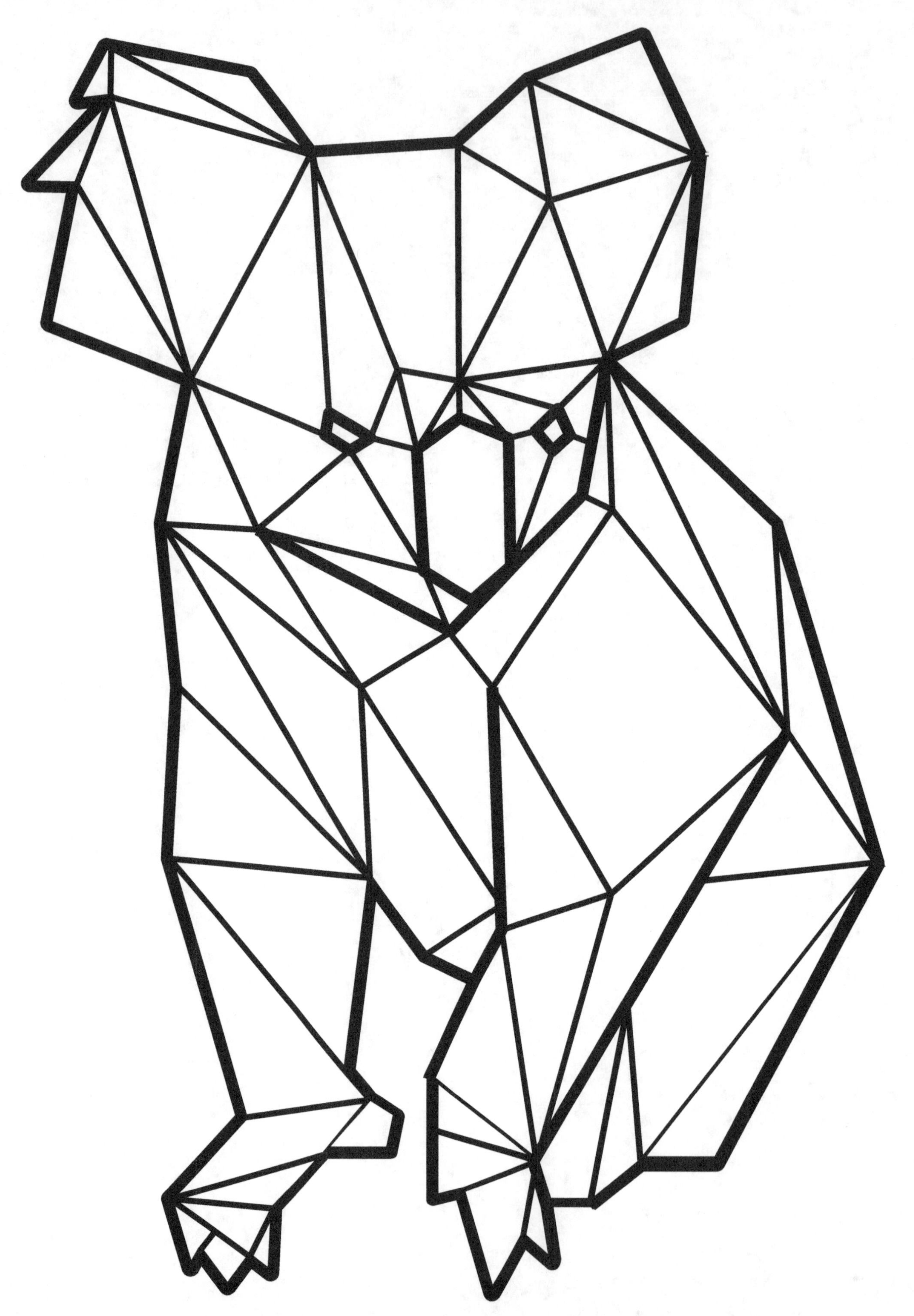

9 798581 904176